Helping teachers
through the edu

Education is messy. It defies attempts to contain it, label it, predict its moves or understand it. It surprises, frustrates, and has numerous different faces, moods and manifestations.

That makes working out what works – or what "works" even means – very difficult.

And yet academics across the world spend their careers trying to "tidy" it all up. Often with little recognition, these researchers work tirelessly within their individual disciplines to find ways of helping teachers in the classroom. Thousands plug away at small sections of the same picture, and that picture then becomes but a dot on a grand pointillist painting of research applicable in education.

Sometimes, academics become "edu-famous" – celebrated by teachers, with their recommendations followed to the letter. Sometimes they are shamefully ignored despite the massive benefits their work may bring. It often seems that luck is a huge factor in terms of which category they eventually fall into.

The aim of the *Tes* Podagogy series of podcasts has been to shine a light on both the edu-famous and the less famous – to scour that education painting

for the research we feel best matches the concerns and interests that teachers tell us about.

Over 18 months, we have been lucky enough to find more than 40 academics who were willing to share their research and break it down for our teacher audience. And that audience has grown to numbers we never expected to reach: more than 30,000 listeners per month.

Just as successful have been these written summaries of those interviews. The first two "seasons" sold out and we have high hopes for this third season, too. There are some fantastic people involved, talking about some incredibly diverse topics.

As long as teachers keep listening and reading, we will keep producing these podcasts and season summaries. There is clearly a desire among the profession to bring some order to the mess, and though the research can never clear it up completely, it can hack teachers a route through the chaos.

We hope you enjoy this series, and remember to keep listening: all our podcasts can be found at bit.ly/Tes_Podagogy
Jon Severs, Tes *commissioning editor*

What teachers need to know about...

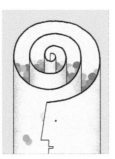

● All transcriptions by Joshua Morris

Chapter one

Professor Angela Duckworth
on character education

Angela Duckworth is the Christopher H. Browne Distinguished Professor of Psychology at the University of Pennsylvania, and founder and chief executive of Character Lab, a non-profit organisation for advancing the science and practice of character development. Her book, *Grit: the Power of Passion and Perseverance*, is a number one *New York Times* bestseller, and her TED talk of the same name is among the most viewed of all time. In this interview, she explains how her work on "character" applies to education.

Much of your recent research has focused on character development. Within this context, what do you mean by 'character'?

For me, "character" includes three types of strength. There is grit (a combination of passion and perseverance for long-term goals, commonly found in high achievers) and self-control, which I've studied as a scientist. I call these "strengths of will".

Then you have "strengths of heart" – empathy, compassion, kindness and generosity – which are really about you relating in positive ways to other people.

Finally, you have "strengths of mind", and those are things like curiosity, creativity and intellectual humility, which enable you to have a really free and fertile life of the mind. I think that all of these strengths are important for kids to develop.

Do you think it is possible to teach these character traits?

There is some debate about whether you can teach these traits or whether people either have them or they don't. Some researchers have suggested that it may be somewhere in between: you can pick these traits up but you can't be taught them in the way you can be taught tennis or calculus. My feeling is that some amount of learning comes from naming these character traits and talking about them in an intentional way, so that is something explicit that teachers can do. But much of the development comes from modelling, which is implicit.

GETTY

Do you think the focus on character is a particularly new thing?
Humility and grit and creativity and gratitude – these are not things that we need for the first time in the 21st century. It's probably since time immemorial that people who want to be good and want to be great need to develop these character traits over the course of their lives.

What can you tell us about the research that is informing your views on character?
One justification for the three-part taxonomy of strengths mentioned earlier is a research study in which we gave hundreds of teenagers questionnaires. For a long list of behaviours, we asked them to say whether this was something they did or didn't do. And we found that there are these three clusters of character strengths that resemble each other. That is to say that when a kid has grit, they are more likely to have self-control. And if you are, for example, grateful, then you are also likely to be someone who has social intelligence. This doesn't work perfectly, but there is a trend. So, this grouping of "heart", "mind" and "will" comes out in the data.

That's one of the studies that motivates our work because it suggests that teachers and headteachers have a three-item checklist. They can ask themselves: are my kids developing in these three important domains? If they're only developing in one,

or even two, maybe there's some attention that needs to be given to what is lacking.

Many teachers and school leaders would support the idea that we need to encourage positive character traits in pupils. But with the curriculum so busy and teachers so time poor, how do we fit this into the classroom?
I don't know a teacher who isn't busy. The idea that you would have to do one more thing means that there is a real hesitation for a lot of teachers and also school leaders [to engage with something like this] and that's completely legitimate.

The question is: how do you do this without making it "one more thing"? One of the ways you do that is modelling. A teacher who is truly passionate about their work, their vocation as a teacher, the subject – that is a big way you teach passion. It doesn't mean your students will necessarily grow up to be teachers, but they will have a visual model and a personal example of what it means to love what you do. That doesn't necessarily take more curriculum time.

In addition to modelling, which is so important, there are other things that wouldn't necessarily take a lot of time. For example, cultivating a "growth mindset" (the belief that you can improve intelligence, ability and performance), which I find in joint work with Professor Carol Dweck to be strongly correlated with grit.

So, when a student makes a mistake or does poorly on an exam, how do you frame the feedback you give them? Do you frame it as 'Oh gosh, this is terrible; you have a real problem here'? Or do you frame it in terms of failure being a necessary part of learning, and say, 'Let's look at exactly what you got wrong and what we're going to do differently next time'?
This is something teachers already have to do: you have to give back quiz [results], you have to give back grades, you have to give feedback on writing. But research suggests that the way in which you give that feedback can dramatically determine whether your student says to themselves afterwards, "I'm a learner, this is part of learning" or "I'm stupid and I'm not a maths person and this isn't for me". So, that's something that doesn't necessarily take curriculum time, but it does take some investment and commitment from teachers.

Surely support from leadership is important, too, because one teacher trying to do it with a class of students is probably going to be far less effective than if it's a whole-school effort?
The idea that a teacher can shut their door and become the determinant of what goes on in the classroom is true and false. To some extent, teachers have a lot of autonomy and freedom but I think it makes a huge difference whether an administration undermines what a teacher is trying to do,

versus supporting and enabling them. I also think that schools have cultures. Morale can be high and morale can be low, school-wide. The most successful teachers I have studied are the ones who feel that their leadership supports what they're doing.

At the moment, you are doing research with schools through your organisation, Character Lab. Tell us about that...
Yes, we have something called the Character Lab Research Network. I know that in the UK, there is a reasonably recent but really robust and admirable tradition of doing research in schools, through the Education Endowment Foundation, through the Behavioural Insights Team and sometimes through both of them working together. I think there's less of that tradition in the US. In a way, we are playing catch up. So, we have a network of schools that have said to us, "we're really excited about this work, in fact, it's what we want to do ourselves". And we're collaborating with those schools to run studies.

Sometimes, it's just a survey study to take the pulse of how happy kids are, how engaged they are, what they find to be meaningful in their everyday lives. And sometimes, we're randomly assigning kids to try different activities designed by scientists and educators to increase motivation or achievement.

This is the dream I have always had as a scientist: how can you take research on meaningful and helpful topics that would benefit kids' lives and make that as frictionless and fast as possible?

What results are coming out of that research so far?
We conducted our first large-scale experiment in January 2018 with 14,000

high-school students, who participated in a variety of different activities.

A "flip of the coin" determined which activity they would get. This enables us to see if any of the activities were helpful, or which of the activities were more helpful than others. We don't have final data back yet so we'll know more by the end of the summer, when all the school records are in and we can analyse the data.

But I will say, it is science. So, unlike someone who is just looking for their programme to be proven effective, for us it's really a question of whether anything that was designed was effective.

It's the first step in a very long journey, I think, to introducing the idea of data and innovation and experimentation (a word that I don't think is often uttered in education): the scientific method, and thinking about things rigorously and, in some ways, dispassionately. The data are what the data are; if the programme doesn't work, it doesn't work.

Do you ever encounter teachers who are resistant to that way of thinking or who have misconceptions about the relevance of applying this type of research to the classroom?

Most teachers want to see good outcomes for their kids. But I think one element of this kind of research that is new and a little bit difficult to swallow, at least for some teachers – for understandable reasons – is that they don't know what activity their students will be getting, and some of the activities might be more helpful than others.

Generally, teachers like to try to give the best thing to their students and just give it to all of them.

The difference in this approach is that we are accepting that we don't actually know,

as a civilisation, the best ways to motivate kids, the best ways to get them to be kind to each other or to take another person's perspective, or to grow intellectually as creative and curious people.

Since we don't know, there has to be some amount of tolerance for experimenting and innovating. And because we don't know, there is this reason to not have all the kids in the class doing the same thing.

When I was a classroom teacher, I never did anything with half my kids that I didn't do with the other half and so that is a bit of a paradigm shift for some teachers.

If you've been in the classroom for a very long time and you're used to a certain way of doing things, it can be challenging to have a completely new way suggested to you, which is still an experiment and which you don't have proof will actually work for this group of students.

But if a teacher takes a moment to think about what they actually do in their own classroom, there's tonnes of experimentation. You try a lesson plan one way and you realise, at the end of that class, that it's really not going as well as you would have liked.

And then maybe if you're, for example, a secondary school teacher, your new class files in and you tweak [the lesson plan] a little bit. You think, "well, that story fell flat, let me try this other approach".

So, the idea of experimentation isn't really new. I think it's the idea of closing the loop and doing it systematically with measures and statistics that is new. But really, innovation and experimentation is what every teacher has to do. We're just hoping to do it in a more cumulative way.

There are so many things that teachers figure out work for them. But they never get to tell other teachers what they did and why it might have worked because teachers

tend to not have that medium. Scientists, on the other hand – that's kind of what they do: they have a hypothesis, they test whether it works or not, then, hopefully, write it up and tell the world so that the insight can be shared.

What's next for your research into character education? Where would you like to see this work go?
My dream is that, at some point in the not-so-distant future, every child will experience a psychologically wise teacher and that every home has a psychologically wise parent in it.

By that, I mean adults who really understand the way motivation and attention and interest, and traits such as grit and empathy, work as a child is developing.

And in so far as they do understand this better, based on science and how development works, that they're doing a better job of raising kids to develop these character strengths of heart, mind and will. That's the dream.

How do we get there? I think we do a lot more research in schools than we ever have before. And then we do a much better job

than we are now of communicating those scientific insights to parents and teachers. We're not locking them up in hard-to-read scientific journals; we're translating science into practice, so that all kids have a chance to thrive.

Looking back on your time as a maths teacher, how do you think you would have changed your classroom practice if you had known about this research at the time?
As a teacher I was pretty well-intentioned; I think most teachers are. But I was pretty clumsy when it came to, for example, getting my kids to do their homework or getting them to just be nice to each other.

And if I'd had a better understanding of self-control, for example, instead of just nagging kids to do their homework, I would have given them strategies; for example, put your homework out where you can see it, put away distractions (in my day and age it was a television and video games but now it's mostly mobile phones).

Those are things that I didn't know about and I think I would have been a lot more effective in doing what I intended to do if I had known about them. I knew at the time, I had an intuition that I could do it better. But I just didn't know how.

This is an edited version of an interview that was first published in September 2018, bit.ly/DuckworthonCharacter

FURTHER READING
- Character Lab: characterlab.org
- *How Children Succeed: Grit, Curiosity and the Hidden Power of Character*, Paul Tough (2013)
- *Character Education in UK Schools*, James Arthur et al (2015)

Chapter two

Professor Courtenay Norbury
on developmental
language disorder

Courtenay Norbury is professor of developmental language and communication disorders at University College London. She has been at the forefront of efforts to define and better publicise developmental language disorder (DLD), which impacts – on average – two children in every classroom. In this interview, she explains what we know about DLD and offers practical advice for how we might support children who have a DLD diagnosis.

There will be many teachers who do not know what DLD is. Shall we start with a brief overview?

Developmental language disorder is the term used when children are not developing language as you would expect them to be. So, they tend to use shorter utterances, they might have trouble remembering what you have said or understanding what you have asked them to do. And they might use non-specific vocabulary. This results in difficulties in communicating with others.

In our research, we looked at how many children starting school would qualify for a diagnosis of DLD – meaning their language was not at age-related expectations and there was no other reason that might be the case – and we found it was roughly two children in every classroom with very significant language need.

You can usually start to see these challenges with language prior to school entry but, certainly, from school entry, they tend to be quite persistent.

What these students say in a lesson will be less complex, they tend to have more trouble learning words, particularly from context because they don't understand the context of the reading. They won't have very complex grammatical structures in their sentences or their output.

Is this something that is easy to spot?

What a teacher will tend to see is a child having difficulties with learning (they will not be progressing as you would like them to be), who might also have difficulties with peers, who might have difficulties with behaviour and difficulties with reading. That teacher may not always think that what is happening is a language problem, but very often it is.

It sounds like a complex diagnosis?

It's true that children who aren't developing language is a red flag for a lot of things. Usually, by the time children are starting to learn to read, somebody recognises that this child isn't able to access the curriculum or do the things that we're asking them to do. Recognising that a child isn't learning – teachers are pretty good at doing that. Knowing that language is the root of the issue is a little bit harder.

Complicating the issue is that it's very rare to see children who have isolated language problems, so most children who have language problems might also have motor incoordination or attention deficit disorder, and they are likely to have reading problems. That can make a precise diagnosis quite difficult. But usually, by Year 3, most people have identified the fact that language is the problem and then they start looking for ways to support that.

Is recognition of language disorders a barrier to getting that support sooner?

Unlike autism or dyslexia, language disorders do not get a lot of recognition. Often, if I say "dyslexia" or "autism", people will say "oh, yes, I've heard of t hat, my cousin has this". With language difficulties, you don't get that recognition and one of the reasons that we have this

things about parents. Let's be clear: parents don't cause language disorder.

Labelling is relatively controversial, though: some say you should just react to the child in front of you. But do you see the DLD label more as a starting point for teachers?
Absolutely, and I think parents benefit from having a label as well as it gives them something that they can look for further information on and means they can be directed to particular services. It is a kind of shorthand for saying, "this is a problem that needs to be addressed and the most likely thing you will need to focus on is language".

One of the fascinating aspects of this that you have talked extensively about elsewhere is the crossover between language problems and behaviour – that poor behaviour may be down to an underlying language issue?
It might be and it is likely to be influencing that behaviour. Children with language disorder very often don't understand particularly complex instructions and they might therefore not remember all the elements of what you've asked them to do. So, they're not complying with what you've asked them to do and the assumption often is that they've just been naughty, whereas the child may simply not have understood what you have asked them to do.

failure of public recognition is because there are lots of different terms about, so some people might say "language difficulties", other people would say "specific language impairment".

We had a campaign, led by Professor Dorothy Bishop, which was really to get consensus on language difficulties in the field, and it involved educators, parents, speech and language therapists, and researchers. It was really to say "can we get an agreement on terminology and some agreements on diagnostic criteria?". So, that's how we settled on [the term] DLD.

Does the lack of recognition and also the broad span of 'symptoms' mean that parents are often unfairly blamed for failing to provide the right environment at home?
Yes, a lot of people assume that it is poor parenting. Indeed, when we write an article for a newspaper about language disorder, you can see the comments underneath and they're really just saying terrible

Also, behaviour is communication. So, if you can't express your need, or someone has misunderstood you, or you've misunderstood what's going on, sometimes children have no option but to express that in another way. So, a child may want a truck that another child is playing with, and usually a child will negotiate for that truck or ask for it. A child with DLD will not:

they do not have the language skills and tend to lash out, take the truck and run.

That child is usually labelled as naughty when it might be that the child doesn't have any other language skills that will enable him to get the thing that he wants.

Do we know yet why DLD occurs?

We haven't a really good answer for the moment. We know that DLD is influenced by genetic vulnerabilities. I guess the way I think about it is that this is a developmental disorder: the brain is developing differently in a way that makes language learning more challenging.

So, most children with language disorders definitely have problems with verbal memory, but the extent to which that is language or memory is tricky. Some studies have shown that those memory deficits occur in non-verbal domains, other studies don't show that. Speed of processing is an interesting one – we're actually looking at that with our data and what we're finding is that speed of processing isn't causally related to language disorder but it seems to be a marker for different development.

Does this lack of a known cause have an impact on how far we are able to develop effective interventions to support these students?

You can train particular skills and kids can get better at using these skills. But whether that can be used to completely change developmental trajectory, I don't think we have evidence for that yet. So, there is a lot of work still to be done.

I would say that's true for most developmental disorders – it's very definitely work in progress. You can make changes, you can help children to make some progress, you can help them to learn new things about language, and by doing that, help them with their general learning. But curing language disorder, I think, is a long way off.

Is this something only primary teachers have to be aware of?

Definitely not, this is an ongoing problem. All the evidence suggests that language is fairly stable and language disorder is persistent. You can make a lot of progress in primary school, but it is very likely that those children will be going into secondary school and still have quite a big gap between them and their peers, and they're likely to have even more trouble because the nature of the language you need to be successful in secondary school changes a lot. It is very abstract and you're using much more formal structures to make academic arguments, and it just becomes much more difficult for them.

Is it important to talk to pupils with DLD about what might work for them, then?

Absolutely. If you ask children with DLD, they often say "the hardest thing is that people think I am stupid when I just can't explain myself and can't express myself quickly". I think that it is a real problem. When you have somebody who's taking a long time to formulate an utterance and it's not a very complicated utterance, the assumption would be that they're just not very bright. That is not the case for most children with language disorder.

So, it is important to remember that those children with DLD will find written language very difficult as well, so looking at other ways to tap into that knowledge would be fantastic. For these kids, schools can be quite hard because there are so many things they find difficult all the time. So, if there is a way to find something that they

do well and celebrate that, it can really help their self-esteem and their willingness to engage in the things that are more tricky.

Would earlier intervention make a difference for children with DLD?

In our study, we found that, in Year 1, about half the children that we identified as having DLD had been referred to speech and language therapy.

Why not all?

Part of the reason may be around a teacher understanding that the problems that they see are language related. Some of it is around speech and language therapy provision – so, if it takes nine months to get an assessment, then teachers might be reluctant to refer; some of it is about the fact that the diagnostic process is quite stressful for parents and, at that stage, some might not be ready – they might be thinking more that school might help. By Year 3, as I said earlier, most of the kids that we identified had at least received some service.

What can we do early on to try to reduce that gap before children get to school?
I think that, before the age of 5, there are just a lot of natural variations in children's language abilities.

So, one of the things that's been challenging is that, if you're trying to diagnose language disorder in a three-year-old, for about half of the kids you could diagnose, they will be fine by the time they get to school, even if you don't do anything. That's because, like learning to walk, these children may just get language later. So, that makes it difficult to make a good diagnosis early on.

It is difficult, because when you can make the diagnosis more clearly is when it is harder to change the direction of travel.

What is your advice to teachers, then?
I actually think that teachers do a great job of teaching children and that they can differentiate enough to support those kids who are at the bottom.

The difficulty is closing the gap and so, for teachers, often where they can be most helpful is providing scaffolds and support that allow children to participate.

For example, if you are going to have a tricky lesson, to flag for those [DLD] children the words that they're going to need to know and help them – with the support staff in the room – to learn those words. This means that when they hear them in a lesson, they understand, they can keep up with what's going on.

There are children who are probably on the borderline, where very targeted

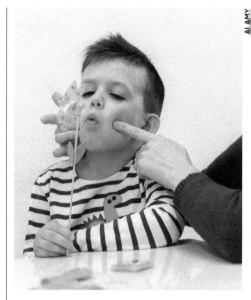

interventions will be enough to keep them learning, and there is a proportion of kids where I think extra help is necessary.

In those cases, it is thinking about how teachers can work together with speech and language therapists to consider, "what is it we need for this child right now?".

It might be something curriculum-based or it might be that the child has no friends – so, it's about really working together to figure out what the priority is for that child at that point in time and getting some specialist support to address those needs.

This is an edited version of an interview that was published in June 2018, bit.ly/Norbury_Language

FURTHER READING
- *Tes* feature on developmental language disorder, bit.ly/Suffering_DLD
- Scales study, www.lilac-lab.org/scales

Chapter three

Professor Steve Higgins
on how much we really know works in education

Professor Steve Higgins is fellow of the Wolfson Research Institute for Health and Wellbeing and professor in the School of Education at Durham University. He was one of the creators of the Education Endowment Foundation (EEF) Teaching and Learning Toolkit and is one of the leading education researchers in the UK. In this interview, he discusses whether we will ever really know what works in education.

Education research is being scrutinised more closely than ever before. Could you give us an idea of the different types of research happening?

Most research and studies tend to be descriptive or developmental, looking at how children learn – for example, how they learn maths or how they learn to read.

Randomised controlled trials (RCTs) [in which subjects are randomly assigned to one of two groups: either the experimental group, which experiences the intervention being tested, or the control group, which experiences the conventional method] are still relatively rare.

In the UK, they are more common than globally, owing to the work of the EEF. I think RCTs have an important place in education research. When you really want to find out whether something makes a measurable difference, then RCTs can do that because you can actually work out whether or not you think this has benefited the particular intervention group compared with the control group.

Can you give us an idea of where a lot of education research happens? You would think it should happen in schools but a lot of it seems to be lab-based?

Yes, historically, education research has been a bit of a hybrid between field and lab

studies, which has very much come from psychology. Of course, academics want to try to control the variables and the conditions as much as possible, to make it as scientific as possible. It is much easier to do those sorts of studies in a lab.

The danger there is that, if you control for all the internal variables in the study, you make it less applicable to the real and hectic world of classrooms, where schools are unpredictable places and you cannot control all the variables. So, you're actually probably learning something that is different in what you might characterise as a field trial as opposed to a lab study.

Lab study is useful in exploring some of the theoretical components, thinking conceptually about what it is you're looking at or studying, but when you move into a field trial in schools in the real world, you want a much better idea of whether this is practical, whether it makes a difference and, if so, how much.

From that, you can learn whether or not you think it is worth trying this approach in other settings that might be similar.

This is an unusual approach, I guess, and it is expensive, so you could not test everything this way, but unless you do test some things this way, you run the risk of always assuming you know what is effective without really knowing how much difference it makes.

Do you think there are areas of current research where this process has perhaps not been followed, where schools are taking up ideas that have not been properly tested in the field?

There are two really clear examples in psychology research. One would be memory where, of course, you want to control and understand the variables in

ALAMY

relation to visual memory, auditory memory, spaced practice, retrieval...you want to design a study where you've controlled those variables for the lab. But in a school, you want to answer a slightly different question, which is "what is the best way to get children to remember a particular skill or content, so that children can use it to be successful in school?" and that is rather more complicated, I think.

Similarly, with motivation studies, there's a lot of work on motivation in psychology, and what we discover there is that you can isolate and define all the variables in the lab but, when those concepts reach schools, you get the messiness of the real world, and personalities and teachers' skills, and it becomes more complicated again.

Even if you did have a series of very rigorous lab studies, you still need to do translational research to understand which of those are actually useful constructs or concepts for the classroom, and not all of them will be, as we're starting to discover – particularly [in terms of] motivation. We also discover the same things around spaced practice or retrieval practice.

You mentioned RCTs earlier as a crucial part of the education research puzzle, but they are relatively controversial: people have criticised them for being unethical in that they potentially give the intervention group an advantage that the control group is denied?
Well, we have no idea whether [most things in education] work or not, but we're quite happy to subject children to them anyway.

So, the default position is actually a bit unethical. That does imply that we genuinely do not know that whatever we are testing will work, in order to make [RCTs] ethical, but given that we don't know how effective most things are in education, I think that is a relatively ethically strong position to take.

These are important issues and you do have to consider whether or not, in a trial, one group might be advantaged in terms of the outcomes if the trial is successful. On the other hand, in the beginning of the trial, we don't really know so, to me, it's worth the risk trying to find out if [something is] beneficial or not, and then using that evidence to try to improve the outcomes for other children.

In terms of design, you can have weightless designs, where you run a trial then, at the end, make a judgement about whether or not it's successful and, if it is successful, you repeat the intervention for the control group – that's one way of approaching it. My reservation about that is, although it is then ethically fair to the children involved in the trial, it removes any way of finding out whether or not the long-terms benefits of a trial are also worth exploring.

So, we know that it's successful at the end of three months but we don't know so much about whether it's beneficial at the end of the year or two years. A good example of

Tes RESEARCH

that, for me, would be the argument about early reading. We don't know so much about how the long-term outcomes of phonics are in terms of reading comprehension and enjoyment of reading.

I would want to reserve the possibility to find out other things by maintaining those control groups over time – at least for a year or two – so you can start to assess what your outcomes are. We know very little about long-term effects in education, so I prefer designs where you keep control and experimental groups intact, if you can follow up long-term outcomes.

Is there a risk at the moment, with the research-informed movement, that the same schools keep popping up in the field studies? Are there schools that will never be touched by research study because it is not on their radar?

That's a really good point because one of my worries is that we have a self-selecting group of schools that volunteer for trials, which are the ones that are trying to improve anyway, and they're looking for different ways to help the children in their care. That might bias your results to working with willing groups of schools – I think that's almost certainly the case.

Ideally, you would want to randomly select schools to be involved in intervention from all populations of schools in England, but that is just not practical for all kinds of reasons: distance, travel and cost but also the ability of schools to engage with a request in a particular trial. So, I think we have to follow the approach that we have, and that means we have to be a bit cautious about generalising from the findings in terms of what's likely to be beneficial. Will it work in other similar schools and how do you define "similar" schools?

How important is teacher bias for a given approach? Is there a danger that a trial becomes skewed by a teacher engaging with, or not engaging with, an intervention?

Yes, that's completely true. I've always argued that you could give me the best researched phonics intervention in the world and I could guarantee to make it fail in my class if I didn't believe in it. That's where the analogies with medicine – and, certainly, pharmaceutical approaches – break down. Because who is actually taking the tablets for the intervention? Effectively, the teacher takes them on behalf of the pupils, and that is a very odd way of thinking about education interventions.

That's also why I believe passionately about the outcomes of research being to inform teachers' choices about what they might want to do, rather than to inform policies and prescriptions about what everyone should do. If we can encourage teachers to think about research and what would work in particular circumstances, you're more likely to get them to opt in to trying those interventions, and that will improve the likelihood of those interventions being successful within their context.

What should teachers be asking the academics running a trial they are involved in?

They will want to know about how to make it practical and feasible in the classroom. Personally, I think that it is also important to have a bit of understanding about why you're doing things, as well as what to do, because that helps you to work out how to respond to pupils in different circumstances, how to manage and prioritise things in a lesson. Again, that's back to schools being hectic and complex in the course of the day.

When we first started working with the EEF, people said that we wouldn't be able to do trials at scale in education: the school would find them too difficult, they wouldn't be practical, there would be too many difficulties in running them, as well as the ethical issues we talked about before.

Actually, most teachers are willing to be part of trials. At the beginning, of course, everyone wanted to be in the intervention group. Now, I think there's a better understanding that, for a fair test, you just have to accept that you'll be allocated to one or the other and, if you're keen then, over time, sign up for more trials and, at some point, you'll be in the intervention group.

Do teachers do what you tell them to? Are they reliable test participants?
That varies a lot by intervention or by what's being tested. Sometimes, it is relatively easy, sometimes it's actually quite hard to explain. With [growth] mindset, for example, everyone thinks they know what it is but, actually, what we discovered in the trial was that, with the teachers who just had the CPD, it didn't have much impact, whereas the group that had the CPD and some support in turning it into lesson materials...there's an impact in that group.

So, working out what level of support, what level of information and the level of practical guidance is actually one of the hardest parts of designing a very good trial.

You've described some complex variables and designs to ensure research finds the answer to the questions it asks, so is this push to have more teacher-researchers really practical, in terms of reliable answers at the end?
That's a really interesting question. I've always thought about this in terms of

"engaging with" and "engaging in" research; those are two helpful distinctions.

All schools and all teachers should be engaging with research and understanding what it says.

We need research to start to challenge some of our perceptions or some of our innate biases, in terms of understanding what's successful [in the classroom]. I think "engaging with" is essential.

"Engaging in" is a bit more complicated. Teachers' first job is to teach and to teach well, and you wouldn't want a lot of their time and energy being taken up in managing research processes, if that disadvantages the learning taking place in their classrooms. That's not always an easy balance to achieve.

On the other hand, there are also some things that schools might want to test out to see whether it works for them in their particular circumstance.

You could design micro trials, in marking, for example: that's a very interesting area and a hot topic in the moment. In school, you could design a micro trial across three classes, where teachers are randomly assigned a particular level or type of marking – or even different assignments and rating – to see whether or not it makes a difference with the individual children. That would be relatively easy to do; it wouldn't necessarily take a lot more time.

This is an edited version of an interview that was first published in September 2018, bit.ly/Whatweknow

FURTHER READING

- Five things you need to know about research, bit.ly/5ThingsResearch
- *Tes* talks to...Steve Higgins, bit.ly/Talk_Higgins

Chapter four

Professor Lucy Cragg
on the role executive function
plays in the classroom

ucy Cragg is associate professor in the Faculty of Science at the University of Nottingham. Her main research focus is cognitive control and the processes that underlie the ability to control thought and actions (also termed executive functions).

These include manipulating and selecting relevant information in working memory, ignoring distractions, suppressing inappropriate response tendencies and flexibly shifting between different tasks.

In this interview, she discusses how her research applies more broadly to learning and education.

Could you start by giving us a primer about what exactly we mean when we use the term 'executive functions' and whether it is the same thing as 'cognitive control'?

You can pretty much use the two terms interchangeably. However, teachers might be more familiar with the term "executive functions". These terms describe the set of skills that we use to control or adapt our behaviour.

Some people have likened it to an air-traffic control system or being the conductor of an orchestra, where you are drawing on the resources of the brain and coordinating them towards the goal that you want to achieve.

For example, in a classroom, a teacher might give a child a task, and the child has got to keep that task's goal in mind.

They've got to ignore anything going on – either internally or externally – that might distract them from that goal, and they've also got to be flexible and adapt their behaviour.

Lots of people split executive function into three sub-groups of processes: working memory, which is holding information in mind and using that information in your head or holding it there in the face of distraction; inhibition, which is the ignoring of distraction in all its forms, whether it be information in the environment or in terms of suppressing responses or actions that are not appropriate in that situation; and shifting or flexibility, which is if they are doing a task and it is not going well, being able to shift to a different tack to try to find a way around the problem.

We know that these skills are very highly related but that they also can be separable, so some children might have good working memory but poor flexibility, for example.

Working memory is an area that is getting a lot of focus and people seem to want to put a figure on the number of chunks of information someone can hold in their working memory. Often, it is five to seven things that is quoted. Is there any accuracy in those numbers?

That's a kind of rough guide. It would refer to five unrelated items – for example, ball, cup, dog, golf, spoon, would be the sort of thing they would give you in psychology studies – but the number varies hugely, so a five-year-old might be able to hold two items in his or her mind and then that develops to the mid teenage years.

And in a classroom there is likely to be a huge variation. In an average Year 4 classroom, some children will be able to hold three or four things in mind, but some may have a working memory capacity similar to a five-year-old.

Also, it depends if these items are related, as you can chunk items together and hold much more. So, there is a rough rule, but there is a lot of variation.

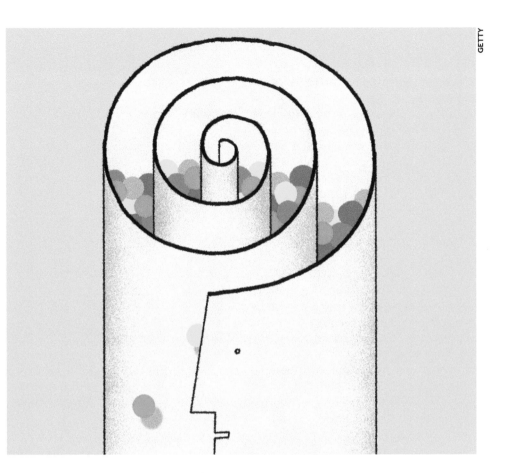

Do we know what, in particular, may be more distracting then other things for children in school?

There is always so much going on internally and externally, and we do not know at an individual level what might be distracting and what will not.

What we do know is that, for anyone, someone calling your name is distracting. We also know that, if something is particularly relevant to you in your life at that minute, then it is going to be more distracting for you than for someone else.

As you get older, you are going to get better at ignoring distractions, but it's not a kind of maturation timetable − it will be affected by experience and practice.

So, when children are in the youngest stages of schooling, is executive function quite an underdeveloped area?

As a general rule, there is usually quite a big increase in executive functions between the ages of 3 and 4: children are suddenly much more able to show inhibitory control and also to shift their focus.

The ability to suppress an inappropriate response happens a bit earlier, but the ability to ignore sounds, noises, things suddenly popping up in front of you − that can take a lot longer. You don't get to adult levels until adolescence.

Is it more likely, then, that to engage children in a task when they are younger, it would be useful for that task to be related in some way to what they like doing or are interested in?
Yes, it would probably influence it. So, children's attention is going to be driven by what they like. If they are interested in it, then it is going to be easier for them to pay attention because they're not going to be as easily distracted by other things.

Are there ways of picking up on whether a particular area of executive function may not be working as well as it could be for that age group? Are there particular disorders related to executive function problems?
If you look at a whole range of developmental disorders, such as autism, attention deficit/hyperactivity disorder (ADHD), and specific learning difficulties such as dyslexia, executive function difficulties are really common across all of these. With any child who is struggling in the classroom, there is likely to be some element of an executive function problem.

So, it is not the cause of those problems, but it's a factor within each of those things that you've just described?
Yes, it's been for a long time associated with ADHD, where there is a particular problem with inhibition, but we now know there are a whole range of different difficulties children with ADHD have, and executive function might be one of them.

People are becoming more aware, but it is definitely not widely known that executive function may be a factor in many classroom

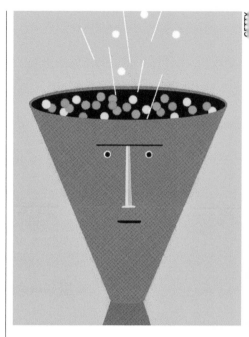

problems. A few years ago, we surveyed teachers on their knowledge of executive function skills and how they related to maths problems. We found that teachers do know what these skills are and that they're important, but they are not familiar with the term "executive function". That formal knowledge – that these skills are important and related to the classroom – is just starting to come through.

Is there a test for executive function?
There are a whole range of different tests that research psychologists and practising psychologists use to measure executive function skills. But you've got to measure in the context of something else. So, if you're testing working memory, you've got to test working memory for something. If you are testing a child's working memory using numbers, and the child also has difficulties understanding numbers, he could

be failing for that reason, as well as the working memory problem. You do have to be careful when you're using these tests.

Do these children often get missed as having potential problems, then?
Definitely, these children often look like they're not trying: they may be just staring out of the window, it may seem like they are not really bothering, but there can be this underlying problem.

If these children are identified as having some issues with executive function, are there specific interventions that have been proved to work?
No, unfortunately this is a kind of holy grail of the research. We know that these skills are very important in the classroom and for learning, but actually trying to pinpoint interventions that can work – there's still a lot of work to be done.

With the working memory training, we know brain training games do improve working memory but that doesn't necessarily transfer to improvement in maths, for example. Similarly, there aren't that many other executive function interventions that have been developed, other than practice on certain tasks, so again, this doesn't seem to transfer that well.

One approach for teachers may be to generally increase awareness, so they are conscious of the executive function and working memory demands in the classroom. For example, it might be in the way you first introduce the topic that you want to minimise executive function demands.

Executive function will have an impact on all areas of a child's learning, so if they have problems with the basic building blocks, then that's going to impact how they're learning maths and reading, in terms of their basic organisation. And if a child seems to be struggling across the board, then this could be an area that has difficulties.

Does that mean minimising distraction, so having a very controlled classroom with little noise and clear directions to the class as a whole?
That is really a key question. In research, because of the controlled nature of the what lots of researchers do, we will just be looking at one aspect at a time: are you better learning in a busy classroom or in a quiet classroom? That may lead to one conclusion but then, if you're not building on [a child's] interests, they might be more easily distracted. So, we don't have that answer.

Could it be that some of the behaviour issues we see in schools are down to executive function problems?
If you have a problem in suppressing impulsive responses then, however much you know you are not supposed to do something, in the heat of the moment, you might not be able to physically control your behaviour. I don't know if people have looked at excluded students and tested for executive function. But it might be very difficult to get a true test because of the difference between lab-based and real-world tests.

This is an edited version of an interview that was published in July 2018, bit.ly/ExecutiveFunctionCragg

FURTHER READING
● *Tes* feature on memory,
  bit.ly/HowMemoriesAreMade
● *Tes* feature on making learning stick,
  bit.ly/RetrievalPractice
● *Tes* focus on executive function,
  bit.ly/FocusExecutive

Chapter five

Professor Paul Kirschner
on why our ideas about
direct instruction are wrong

Paul Kirschner is a distinguished professor at the Open University of the Netherlands. He is one of the world's leading researchers in instructional design. In this interview, he argues that the common perception of direct instruction is inaccurate, and says the research proves that, in reality, this method makes for the most effective teaching.

Direct instruction has a number of connotations in UK education, but do you think we are all talking about the same thing? What do you define it as?

I often use the term "explicit instruction". Learners are novices, and the best way to help them to gain knowledge, skills and understanding is to make sure they get proper instruction.

The first thing to do is you have to set the stage for learning. You have to make sure learners have the prerequisite knowledge, that would also mean creating a learning context for them, so they can contextualise what they're learning.

After you do that, you have to make sure there is a clear explanation of what is expected of them and what you want them to do. This is not giving them algorithms that they have to do but to give them the procedural knowledge to carry out what they are doing. Working with new experience and facts is very difficult in terms of cognitive load, so you have to make the extraneous load as small as possible.

The next thing that you might want to do is modelling. To model the process, show how something is done, walk and talk the students through it in terms of not only showing it but doing it, then trying to explain not only what you did but why you did what you did. Then comes practice. The practice should be guided, which then gradually gives way as the learners become more and more capable of carrying it out themselves.

Next is to do independent practice, and you only do that if you're confident that the student will be fairly successful.

Finally, assessing it – formally, informally and formatively at the end but also formatively throughout. That is how I see explicit instruction.

Is that the definition, or understanding, used in research on direct instruction?

There are a number of different definitions but you could say many share a certain basis with each other. However, there are some that are completely strange. I can't say it in any other way!

You have to realise that, in different situations, you need to use different approaches. I often compare teaching to being a chef in a Michelin-starred restaurant. A good instructional designer or a teacher has techniques, tools and ingredients and he or she uses them to prepare tasty, good-looking and healthy meals for clients. A good chef doesn't limit himself or herself to just one tool, one technique or one ingredient – and neither should the teacher.

The teacher should be making use of all the techniques, tools and ingredients that he or she has to achieve effective, efficient and enjoyable learning

So you could say "direct instruction" is "any academic instruction led by a teacher". It's completely non-specific: it could be discovery learning led by the teacher or it could be a lecture led by the teacher.

Or you could say that direct instruction is a lecture and passive listening: it is authoritarian, drill and skill, it is isolated work, it focuses on tests, it is one-size-fits-all. This is a straw man that is very easy

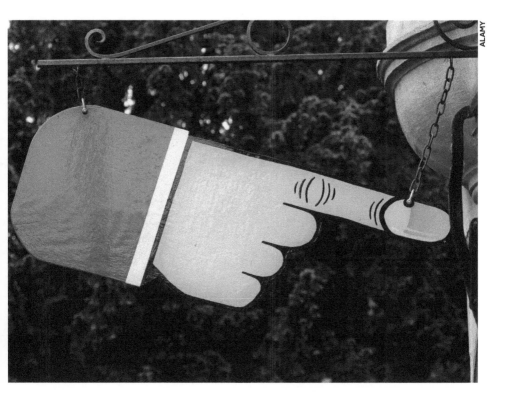

to knock down. I don't think either of these is right. Direct instruction can best be seen as "certain procedures used by effective teachers", as mentioned earlier.

Within the tenets of direct instruction that you identify, it seems educators have a lot of freedom to interpret teaching in different ways?
Yes, teachers are not only experienced, they're experts. They have a deep conceptual knowledge, both of the domain that they are teaching in but also in the domain of teaching. They know the tools, techniques and ingredients that they can use.

The teacher is capable of thinking on their feet, being very flexible and adaptable. So, yes, within the process, there is quite a lot of flexibility, if you hold on to those basic commonalities.

Does that make research into direct instruction difficult because, although you have those constraints and you can try to isolate those elements in your study, the delivery plays a big part in the effectiveness of the approach?
Definitely. But almost all education is difficult because it's very hard to control for many of the confounding factors.

Even if I do the exact same thing, the first lesson period in the morning can be completely different from the second lesson period in the morning. So, anything you're doing in education means that you have to do your best knowing that you'll never be evidence-based. I tend to use the phrase "evidence-informed". In education, there are too many other factors.

The way one teacher approaches and carries out a lesson in direct instruction is different from another teacher, the rapport between one teacher in a class and another, the way they take care of their class – all these things are completely different. It makes it hard to carry out that type of research. In a laboratory setting, it's a lot easier, but there are people who do not carry out the steps in doing good empirical research that they should be carrying out.

What you cannot do is say, "We did one experiment, this worked, so it will always work." Something that works with college students probably won't work with primary schoolchildren. Something that works in one domain possibly won't work in another. So, you have to be very careful in the claims that you make.

With all this taken into account, you are still certain that direct instruction is the most effective way of teaching?
Yes, we can say that. I mean, if you look at what John Hattie did with his book, *Visible Learning*, he found, in 304 studies, that the average effect size [of direct instruction on learning outcomes] was almost 0.6, which is incredibly large, and one of the largest of any of the interventions that he studied.

If we look at Project Follow Through, which was carrying out in the US in the 1970s and 1980s, with something like 70,000 students, they found that direct instruction had far and away the best results for language, spelling, maths and reading.

Even in the latest results from the Programme for International Student Assessment (Pisa), if you look at the factors associated with science performance – outside of the socio-economic profiles of the learners, which have an incredible effect upon how well learners do – the index of teacher direct instruction was, I think, the third most effective strategy, whereas enquiry-based instruction, which is the opposite of direct instruction, was almost one of the worst.

Direct instruction, across the board, is effective and efficient, and has been proven to be such.

So, why is there such animosity in some areas of teaching to this approach – is it a misunderstanding of what it is?
There are possibly three reasons, but I haven't done research on that, so now I'm giving my opinion. And my opinion is as good or as bad as anyone else's opinion on this! The first thing I see, when talking with a lot of teachers, is that it seems that those who embrace direct instruction, or would like to embrace direct instruction, are afraid of being branded as dinosaurs or Luddites – those types of terms.

Second, [direct instruction] is not what the educational gurus propagate as being

what good, modern, progressive education should be. They claim there is a way you should be doing it in the 21st century – I mean, [this idea of] "21st-century skills" is the biggest piece of snake oil that I have ever come across.

The third reason, and we've done a little bit of research on that, is that direct instruction requires a heck of a lot of knowledge from the teachers. There's been quite a lot of research in the previous couple of years as to what knowledge new and upcoming teachers are getting of good teaching and learning strategies, and that tends to be minimal at best.

Is there room, then, for some of the pedagogical approaches that are thought of as being progressive to actually be delivered in accordance with the six tenets of direct instruction you laid out earlier?

Definitely. Let's take group work. The first thing that we have to realise about group work is that most people don't know how to collaborate and coordinate their group work. That means you need,

before you start working in teams, to lay the groundwork for what it means to work in a team.

Second, you have to take the time to properly form the teams. Then, you look at why you want to make use of group instruction and consider what are the specific learning goals? – which is one of the tenets of direct instruction – and you say, "OK, I want to use it for a certain reason; maybe I don't want to use it to help them learn the basic facts within an area but I want to have them use it to work on a task that is larger than they can carry out by themselves".

Then you can make use of working in groups, if you use it for the proper reason.

This is an edited version of an interview that was first published in May 2018, bit.ly/Kirschner_direct

FURTHER READING
- *Tes* focus on…direct instruction, bit.ly/Focus_onDirect
- *Tes* article on research, bit.ly/5thingsaboutresearch

Chapter six

Professor Neil Mercer
on oracy in the classroom

Neil Mercer is emeritus professor of education at the University of Cambridge and director of Oracy Cambridge. He is a leading expert on the role of spoken language in the classroom. In this interview, he discusses the evidence for, and practical strategies to implement, teacher and pupil talk.

When you talk about oracy, what do you mean by that?

I mean spoken language as a distinctively human tool for communicating and creating understanding and its whole range of possibilities. For example, one of the things I am interested in is the relationship between children's experience and use of language, and the development of their thinking and reasoning.

That's where the Thinking Together project, which I began with Rupert Wegerif and Lyn Dawes, came from. We wanted to see whether getting children skilled at thinking collectively and reasoning together in discussions would have a positive effect on how they reasoned alone.

If language is connected to thinking, does that mean that if our spoken language is limited, our thinking skills will also be limited?

There is a lot of evidence now to show that young children's early language experience has a big effect on their academic attainment and, by implication, that it's having some effect on how they are processing knowledge. Language is this tool for thinking on your own as well as collectively.

It's been suggested that a child's social background could affect their chances through the opportunities they've had to develop language skills. And I think we have to admit that. It's not that people are

having no experiences at all. It's whether they are experiencing the range of ways of using language that underpin different ways of thinking.

If they have not encountered a lot of reasoned discussions outside of school, for example, then you can't expect them to have reasoned discussion in their repertoire. And they may not have the internal version of reasoning that this type of discussion is the external model for.

That's why I always say to teachers, especially primary teachers, that they're the only second chance for some children to have that rich language experience. Children might not get it anywhere else.

How important is teacher talk?

Talk is the main tool of a teacher's trade. It's a skill to use it effectively to help children develop. What we know now is that the ways teachers use talk in the classroom make a difference to the quality of students' learning. All the evidence suggests that, to learn well, children need authoritative presentations made by experts – well-qualified, trained teachers, who can explain things in a way that the ordinary person might not do so well.

There's no way around it. There are certain things pupils have got to know and it's the job of the teacher to make sure they know them.

However, if you want the students to develop the ability to work with that knowledge, to reason with it, to practise it and to be able to make it their own, then they need to speak, too.

There's got to be a balance; that's what I am really arguing for. You want the balance between opportunities for sitting and listening and opportunities for dialogue, in which the teacher hears what the pupils haven't yet understood.

Some more traditional teachers would say that, rather than listening to pupils, you could find out what they have understood just from giving them a test. Do you agree?

I don't think you get the same information from a test. From the evidence I have seen and the recordings that I've heard, there is a difference between a child getting something wrong and that child being able to explain what they do and don't understand. Pupils shouldn't just be receptacles of knowledge. They should be speakers of it, so they can operate it and speak it. And that is part of the skill.

You're not going to learn French if all you do is listen, and it's the same for all subjects. It's a case of giving the students the opportunity to get into the discourses of subjects, and make them their own, and the teachers can provide feedback on that.

And when the opportunity is right, the teacher can see much more clearly what still needs to be taught. I am not saying that tests are not useful, but they only give you a certain limited kind of information and they won't give the pupils that chance to construct their knowledge themselves.

So, if you want the best results, in terms of pupils' satisfaction, as well their progress and their exam results, then balance is what we should be striving for.

Does the research suggest what that balance should look like between teacher talk and non-teacher talk in percentage terms?

I don't think it does in any really clear, simple way. Crude proportions aren't really important. What we do know a lot more about now is what kinds of ways of using talk matter.

It's worth pointing out that there aren't any large-scale systematic studies that show that a straight monological approach to teaching works. Likewise, there aren't any studies that show a highly progressive, "let the children discover for themselves" approach works either.

What we do have now are lots of relatively small-scale studies that have been done all over the world that have suggested that certain ways of teachers interacting with students is helpful for their learning.

And in the past year, we have had two of the first large-scale studies in this area: one done by us at Cambridge with Year 6 pupils, and one done at the University of York with Year 5.

In both cases, it was found that teachers who enabled children to participate in discussion, and got them to elaborate their ideas and to question things, got better Sats results in literacy and in maths.

We also know from our study that if the teachers used well-organised group work, where reasoned discussion could take place, then they also got better results. So, those are the sort of things that encourage me to feel that we're not misleading anybody if we say you should strive for this balance between authoritative presentation and genuine dialogue.

And when you're in the dialogue, think about doing specific things: get pupils to elaborate on their ideas; make sure it is not just the usual suspects who answer your questions, but try to get participation widely; get them to discuss each other's ideas. That way, the teacher will not only learn more about what they all think but the pupils will as well.

Do we know what makes teacher talk effective in terms of things like pitch, tone and content?

With pitch and tone, you've got some general rules that apply to presentational talk in any situation, such as clarity of enunciation and not talking too fast. I think we know those things.

In terms of content, what we know is that the best presentations are those that take into account your audience's level of understanding but move them on just a little bit.

It is a very hard thing to say you should do but, if you can be inspirational enough to get people interested, then that is helpful, too.

So, there are lots of fairly straightforward rhetorical and oratory skills that teachers can be taught to use, but a lot of it is having a knowledge of what level of understanding you're working with. This isn't an easy thing to achieve, but it is possible.

The important thing is that teachers are aware of their use of talk. They shouldn't take it for granted and assume that effective talk will happen naturally. It is a skill – it is something that you learn to do. And this is absolutely crucial because talk is the main tool of a teacher's trade.

Does the personality of a teacher make a difference to the effectiveness of teacher talk or how talk in the classroom should be used?

Anybody can learn these skills in a way that will make them better at it. There will still be some people who have a talent for it, if you like, but I am convinced that people can learn. And I don't think you need to be an extrovert. Some of the people I know who are the best teachers are very introverted, but they can teach a whole class marvellously.

The question the teacher's got to ask is what are the needs of the pupils? The proportion of instructive talk, as opposed to dialogue, where pupils are taking a more active role, ought to be determined by what you are trying to achieve rather than by your personality as a teacher.

And I don't think you can achieve all the right outcomes in education by only using one or the other approach – free dialogue or monologue presentation. You need both.

If you have a shy pupil who is reluctant to talk, is forcing that child to speak in public the right thing to do?

Some people are more naturally willing to speak. But the thing about oracy is that the range of skills is quite broad.

In the past, there has been a tendency to think of oracy as meaning speech-making or presentations or taking part in debates. These are the obvious things. But that's not what we really mean by "oracy". We mean the full range of spoken language skills, which would include doing things like working in a team to get something done; it would include listening sensitively

learn to do. That is what I and other people pushing for oracy education are really arguing for. What we are saying is that children should be taught oracy in the same way they are taught literacy, or maths or music.

It's the same as learning a musical instrument: you've got to learn the skills. You can't be a jazz pianist straightaway, you've got to learn the scales. At first, it might be a bit clunky, but you get looser and you get better at it. And that happens through a mixture of being told how, being allowed to develop those skills, and getting feedback and practice.

Unless we create the space for that to happen, you won't get people doing it, and so what we're really saying is that it ought to be explicitly taught.

to someone about something so that you can take account of what they're saying and help them. Children will vary in their profiles. Some will have no worries about standing up and talking, but put them in a group and they never listen to anyone. Meanwhile somebody else might be brilliant in a group and yet be tongue-tied when asked to speak in front of the class.

One of the things that has come up with oracy education is that it shouldn't be a matter of privilege or social advantage. We all know that people who have been to the most elite public schools have no problem interacting and speaking in public – that might be why a lot of them seem to be running the country.

This doesn't happen by accident; those schools actually do, effectively, train pupils in oracy. But in the state sector, oracy has been subdued in favour of literacy and numeracy, and is not seen as important.

What the elite public schools provide are opportunities for pupils to learn those skills, regardless of their personalities. They learn to be comfortable with it, as it is treated as something you can do and something you

Do you think that oracy needs to be formally assessed for teachers to focus on it more?

I think so. My colleagues and I have come around to this idea, reluctantly in some ways, because the minute you assess something, it constrains it, doesn't it? Think about reading comprehension: what are you really assessing? You're not necessarily assessing all the subtlety of what you get from reading.

But, unfortunately, unless something is assessed, it's not taken seriously in our education system. So, that's one reason why I think oracy does need to be assessed. It's a great shame at GCSE that the English oral was lost, because that means that teachers will feel that they shouldn't devote as much time to speaking skills.

That's why we've created an oracy framework and an assessment scheme. We did this for Year 7. It is quite possible to do.

And it helps to have some sort of frame to make this slippery stuff, spoken language, a

bit more visible: so you can see that it has a linguistic element to it, as well as the vocabulary and grammar aspect, but that there's also a cognitive aspect – how well the arguments are being presented, for instance – and a social and emotional one, because I won't convince you of anything if I just sit and shout at you. That's what the framework shows.

Would you take each of those aspects and teach them discretely? Or would you bundle them all into an activity?
You need to do both. The framework shows you that these things are there and it helps everyone to see them. But once you've seen these elements, you're more aware of them yourself and can recognise that some will be more important in certain activities than in others.

For instance, if you are giving a talk to 200 people, your clarity of enunciation, your body language – things like that – will be absolutely crucial. So, those aspects of the framework would come to the fore.

But in group work, it is not so important that you're speaking clearly because I am sitting next to you. Body language is almost irrelevant, but the listening skills and the social and emotional aspect, which are less important in a big presentation, are crucial.

In different situations, clusters of these skills will operate in different ways. Once people see that, it starts to make sense and what you'd hope is that, once you've got a meta level of understanding, you are more in control of your own learning and your own development – you can see what you are striving for.

Do you think that oracy needs to be taught as early as possible?
Yes. Primary children are less easily embarrassed and, if you can get oracy skills and expectations around speaking set in the primary years, then it would be much easier for secondary teachers to build on it, definitely. We've done interventions with Year 1 and Year 2, and it's been great.

If you can bring primary and secondary teachers together on this, you can make sure there's some continuity involved and that it doesn't all get lost, or you have to start again. That's important.

This is an edited version of an interview first published in April 2018, bit.ly/Mercer_oracy

FURTHER READING

- Littleton, K and Mercer, N (2013) *Interthinking: Putting Talk to Work* (Routledge)
- Dawes, L, Mercer, N and Wegerif, R (2004, second edition) *Thinking Together: a programme of activities for developing speaking, listening and thinking skills* (Imaginative Minds)
- Alexander, R J (2017, fifth, revised edition). *Towards Dialogic Teaching: rethinking classroom talk* (Dialogos)

Chapter seven

Professor Victoria Murphy
on research into English as an additional language

Victoria Murphy is professor of applied linguistics at the University of Oxford. She is an expert in English as an additional language (EAL) and bilingualism, and has conducted extensive research into both areas. In this interview, she explains what the research can tell teachers about the best ways of supporting EAL learners.

Is it accurate to say that the proportion of EAL learners in the system has increased significantly in the past decade or so?

That's indeed correct, the proportion of EAL children in primary and secondary has actually doubled in the past 20 years.

The strongest concentrations of EAL pupils are found in London and the Greater London area, and in big metropolitan centres, but it is also true that you will find EAL children around the country: Yorkshire and the Humber has a fairly high proportion of EAL pupils and every teacher is likely to encounter EAL children at some point in their career.

When we say EAL, what do we actually mean? Are there criteria to classify it?

It is a problematic category. It was invented, if you like, for the National Pupil Database (NPD): it's a tag in the NPD essentially. The way it's defined is so general, it really just highlights children who have another language in the home, and that's it.

It doesn't speak to whether and to what extent the child was exposed to English since birth or in any other context.

It doesn't say anything about their proficiency in English and, importantly, it doesn't say anything about their knowledge of their home language or their proficiency in that language. There is a tendency for people to assume that EAL means bilingual or emergent bilingual. But we have found in our research, when we've asked the teachers to identify the EAL pupils, that we have had native speakers of English in those samples.

That often happens because you might have a child who has one parent who speaks French and another who speaks English, but the French parent never speaks French to the other parent or, indeed, to any of the children. Yet that pupil would be tagged EAL in the school system.

Similarly, children who are raised as simultaneous bilingual, so English is one of

their first languages and therefore they've a very high proficiency in English, they would also still be tagged as EAL.

Then you have the child who is just visiting from another country for a short period, they are EAL.

And children who have just arrived in the country – perhaps in terms of a refugee situation or something like that – they are also EAL.

They're all lumped into the same box but I just described very different situations that those children are in – massively diverse – and so, any time that we talk about EAL in general terms, we are really being a bit reckless because we're probably covering up the kinds of complexities that might be relevant for certain subgroups.

Does the use of the term skew a perception of EAL learners detrimentally?

One of the issues I have with EAL is that it is used within the construct of a discussion about deficit, so we automatically assume that if a child is EAL, there is a problem.

Non-EAL children have difficulties sometimes with reading, they sometimes come from disadvantaged backgrounds, sometimes they come to school with weak language and communication skills – just like some EAL children. So, one of the big problems with EAL is the way in which we talk about it generally, as if it's a problem, but it really doesn't have to be. There are a lot of EAL children who are really strong, good at learning, high achievers, good at reading and have no trouble whatsoever.

Are we in danger, with EAL, of promoting a deficit model, then, whereby these children have lower expectations thrust upon them?
Yes, there can be negative connotations to being EAL. And, similarly, some schools might feel that they want to include children as EAL who might be really proficient bilinguals, for other reasons.

We are getting better, because we have such a high proportion of children who are EAL in the English school system. There is definitely an improvement on some levels – we're having this conversation, for example, which we might not have had a few years ago.

But we can do a lot better in terms of initial teacher education and supporting teachers to work with EAL children. There is a lot of complexity there and we need improvement in terms of making better decisions about how we support EAL children who may be struggling.

Does it make any difference, in circumstances where a child has no or little English language, what their native language is?
That's something that we haven't really understood very well. There was a report – commissioned by the Education Endowment Foundation, the Bell foundation and Unbound Philanthropy – that was able to show the subgroups of EAL children who might struggle and, of course, there are particular linguistic profiles of those specific ethnicities. And there are analyses

where specific linguistic subgroups in EAL have been identified as being more or less likely to have higher or lower attainment.

But that's something, from a research point of view, that we don't understand really well.

From a linguistic point a view, there is an interesting paper, published this year, that looked at what they called "linguistic distance" [how different one language is from another] between the languages that the child was developing, and which was able to identify it as an important predictor of the child's vocabulary development.

This is something that, certainly from a research perspective, we need to start looking at carefully to be able to make more

different, there are no false friends: it's very clear, "this is very different, this is something new I have to learn".

But it's premature to be able to identify which languages, which linguistic groups, could potentially create more difficulty for children than others. Generally speaking, if you look at the bilingualism literature, these sorts of distance relationships are not necessarily going to explain why a child might be struggling with literacy, for example.

They might explain particular development trajectories in vocabulary; they might explain specific errors that a child might make as they're developing their linguistic acknowledge. So, yes, we need to look at this more, but I also don't think that is going help us make predictions about education and a child's achievement.

Does it make a difference how many different languages are spoken in a school? We often hear of schools that have 10, 20 or more different languages – does it follow that the more you have, the harder the task of teaching?

The way in which teachers teach EAL children typically – and, again, this is a generalisation – the linguistic background of the child doesn't figure: the concern is the development of English, not the development of their home language.

I think that is the problem, We should be developing their home language, and educational context should be structured so we can promote bilingualism for all sorts of reasons, yet we don't, typically.

Are there any general EAL approaches that the research suggests would work?
There are some specifics and, again, it might vary depending on the child and their particular needs, but one thing that is

informed predictions about where we might expect certain children to struggle.

By 'distance', you mean from English to the mother tongue?
Yes. Linguistic distance is a tricky concept to define – and there are different ways in which to do it – but that's generally the idea.

We don't really have enough research because you could predict that similarity could create difficulty or confusion. For example, you assume something that works [a certain way] in your home language works [the same way] in English, which could sometimes create mistakes. We call them "false friends". Whereas, sometimes, when [the child's languages] are really

really important for all children is that they feel part of the classroom, that they're a valued member.

Unfortunately, a lot of children with EAL come from ethnic minorities and are first- or second-generation immigrants, and there is a lot of unhealthy political rhetoric about immigrants in England at the moment. It's been well documented that there are a number of children with EAL who have been at the very unpleasant end of racial and ethnic abuse. Schools primarily have to make sure that their children from different ethnic and linguistic backgrounds are made to feel safe, well supported and valued.

Has the research focused on pedagogy with EAL?

We've had lot of research done on EAL from different perspectives. We have spent quite a bit of time looking at teachers' perceptions, beliefs and concerns. This research is obviously very important and serves as a springboard for developing other work.

It tends to be from relatively small-scale studies and they attempt to be somewhat descriptive, which is always an important first step in doing research. We have less quantitative and empirical research. I hope we are going to see more quantitative, large-scale intervention-type studies that can really look at what's effective.

The other area that's burgeoning within the EAL world is "translanguaging". It is a bit of a tricky construct – essentially it means drawing from the child's other languages within the English classroom, so they can use those other languages as support while they are doing their work.

How does it work in practice?

If, for example, there was more than one child in that class who spoke Language A,

it would be allowing those children to talk about the maths problem in Language A, as they were trying to work through it.

Obviously, some teachers are a little concerned by that because, if they don't know what their students are saying, they may feel that they've lost control of the situation. But the research tso far has shown there are different ways of managing this sort of pedagogy and I think this is where we need to be going. It is about trusting them: students, by and large want to learn and do well.

Teachers haven't really had any training in this multilingual pedagogy because it is very new but, as it develops, we're going to be in a much stronger position to be able to support effective practice in English schools.

This is an edited version of an interview first published in May 2018, bit.ly/EAL_generalisations

FURTHER READING
- How to save MFL, bit.ly/Save_MFL
- Why total immersion is the best way to teach languages, bit.ly/Total_immersion
- How to ensure your EAL learners are making progress, bit.ly/EAL_progress

9 780995 741577